TRADITIONAL VENETIAN DESSERT RECIPES

Sweet Serene Republic

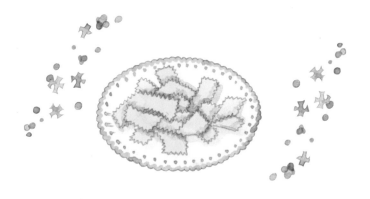

Baìco'li
Za'leti - Ga'lani

arsenale editrice

CONTENTS

SWEET VENICE

Traditional Venetian cuisine boasts a wealth of delicious recipes. Venetian desserts are famed in culinary art as refined and delightful specialities, and are served even at the end of the most elegant menus. And there is such a huge choice! Mention need only be made of the amazing variety of biscuits ensuring such various tastes and shapes as baíco'li, za'leti and buso'lai. Not to forget fried desserts such as "ga'lani" during the Carnival period, "fave dei morti" in Autumn, "pinsa" at Epiphany and "fugassa de Pasqua" for Easter in Spring. As well as tarts, puddings, "rosoli" and desserts based on fruit.

For the most part, these recipes are prepared with simple ingredients generally always available in our larders: flour, butter, milk, eggs, sugar. Some are more sophisticated and others are flavoured with exotic spices recalling the distant times when the Serene Republic traded with the Orient; others still are associated with traditional festivals; and even others are typical of the Jewish culture that was once rooted in the Ghetto area. Some of these desserts may also be found in pastry shops in other parts of the Veneto, while many are exclusively Venetian. It is an impressive selection of tastes and traditions, a world of sweet and refined creativity to be enjoyed deliciously to the full. Discovering the characteristic confectionery of Venice is a delightful way to enjoy fuller harmony with this truly unique city – that without doubt also reveals itself through its "sweet" cuisine.

Editorial co-ordination
Arsenale Editore

Editing
Chiara Scudelotti

Photography
Archivio Arsenale

English translation
Peter Eustace

Traditional venetian dessert recipes
Sweet Serene Repubblic

First Edition January 2009

© ARSENALE EDITRICE

Arsenale Editore Srl
Via Ca' Nova Zampieri, 29
37057 - San Giovanni Lupatoto (Verona, Italy)

BAÍCO'LI
BAÍCOLI

400 g of fine flour, 15 g of beer yeast,
70 g of butter, 60 g of fine sugar, 1 egg white, 1.5 glasses
of fresh milk, salt.

Carefully dissolve the yeast in half a glass of lukewarm milk.
Heap 100 g of flour on a pastry board, dish the top and add the
milk and yeast. Knead into a rather firm dough (add a little
more flour if necessary).

Use a knife to cut a cross on the top and then place the dough
in a bowl, cover and leave to rise for half an hour in a lukewarm place.

Then sprinkle the remaining flour over the pastry board with
the sugar, butter at room temperature, whipped egg white and
a pinch of salt.

Knead this mixture with a little lukewarm milk as required to
prepare a dough resembling bread; split into 4 parts and then

Baíco'li are the most famous Venetian biscuits. These delicate flaky
biscuits were also made by a famous confectionery industry whose
typical tins bore these sweet verses:
> «No gh'è a sto mondo no più bel biscoto
> più fin, più dolce, più lisiero e san
> par mogiar nella cicara e nel goto
> del baicolo nostro venezian»

(The world has no better, finer, sweeter, lighter and healthier biscuit
to dip in cups or glasses than our Venetian "baicolo"). These tins have
now been replaced by cardboard boxes but the tradition of "baíco'li"
biscuits – going back at least 200 years – is still enjoyed today. It
seems that the name derives from a resemblance with tiny mullet, a
fish known in Venetian dialect precisely as "baíco'li".

roll out into pieces 4–5 cm long. Place them on a buttered oven tray well separated from each other so that there enough space for them to rise for the second time and then bake. Leave to rise again for about an hour and a half.

Then place in the oven at 180 °C and bake for about 10 minutes, so that the dough colours without crusting or browning.

Lastly, leave the biscuits to cool and then rest wrapped in a cloth for a couple of days.

Now use a sharp knife to cut them into thin, irregular slices before slightly biscuiting them in a hot oven.

These delicious biscuits can be served with coffee or "zabaione" and keep for a long time in a well–closed tin box or glass container. They are ideal with Recioto di Soave dessert wine.

BUSO'LAI
BUSOLAI

1 kg of fine flour, 50 g of beer yeast,
200 g of sugar, 150 g of butter, the grated rind
of 1/2 lemon, 1/2 glass of dry white wine, salt.

Dissolve the yeast in half a glass of lukewarm water. Add half a glass of flour and knead into a soft dough.

Add a spoon of sugar, a pinch of salt, cover and leave to rise until the dough doubles in volume (this will take about 30 minutes).

In the meantime, melt the butter and then allow it cool slightly before blending it with the risen dough together with the sugar, the remaining flour and the lemon rind.

Pour the mixture on to a pastry board and begin kneading, adding the wine a little at a time until a fine, soft, elastic and uniform consistency is achieved. Form the dough into a ball and then leave to rise for a couple of hours.

Then divide the mixture into small pieces, roll these out in-to cylinders and then form "s–shaped" or "doughnut–shaped" pieces about 8 cm in diameter – in the later case, leaving rather large holes since they tend to close

BAICOLI

BUSO'LA

during baking. Place them on oven paper and bake in a pre–heated oven at 170 °C for about 15–20 minutes until they become golden. Serve cold.

"Buso'lai" – there are many different variants – are very popular in the city of the Doges and are characteristic of the island of Burano (they are also known as "buso'lai buranèi").
Even before the 1800s, the Venetian custom was to enjoy them instead of bread or dipped in coffee and milk. Another very popular custom was to dip them in wine at the end of a meal because it was thought this helped digestion.

BIANCHETI
BIANCHETI

400 g of fine flour, 4 egg whites,
40 g of vanilla sugar, 1/2 a small glass of brandy,
1 small spoon of extra virgin olive oil,
5 g of confectionery yeast, salt.

"Biancheti" are one of the many small doughnuts boasting ancient traditions.

They resemble little cakes also baked in other Italian and European regions.

Use a pastry board to knead the flour, egg whites, vanilla sugar added a little at a time, yeast, pinch of salt, oil and brandy. Knead all these ingredients carefully into a dough with the consistency of bread dough and then continue to knead until rather soft.

Then roll out the dough into pieces about 10 cm long; then join the ends to form small "doughnuts".

Bring a pot of water to the boil, immerse the "biancheti" and wait until they rise to the surface.

Then remove them with a sieved ladle and leave to dry.

Lastly, place them on a buttered oven tray and bake at mode–rate heat.

These delicious biscuits can be served with hot chocolate, coffee or tea.

ZA'LETI
ZALETI

*250 g of fine maize (corn) flour, 250 g of fine flour,
200 g of butter, 150 g of sugar, 100 g of raisins/sultanas,
4 eggs, milk, grated rind of 1 lemon, milk,
vanilla flavouring, icing sugar, salt.*

The name of these typical Venetians biscuits was inspired by the yellow colour of the maize–corn flour, they are also known as "gialletti". They were once a speciality of the Carnival period but are now available in Venetian pastry shops all year round.

Wash the raisins/sultanas and leave them to soften in a little water; in the meantime, beat the eggs with the sugar in a bowl. Mix the two types of flour in another bowl, add a pinch of salt, a dash of vanilla and the grated rind of a lemon. Then mix the two flours, the beaten eggs, knobs of butter at room temperature and the drained raisins/sultanas dried with a cloth.

Knead this mixture, adding a little milk if necessary to soften. Roll out to a diameter of about 6 cm and then cut into pieces of 7–8 cm, shaping them into small ovals.

Carefully butter an oven tray, arrange the ovals on it and bake at 180 °C for about 20 minutes (cooking time may vary depending on the size of the "biscuits").

When baked, remove the tray from the oven, sprinkle the "za-'leti" with icing sugar and leave to cool before serving with chilled Custoza or Vespaiolo di Breganze white wine.

IMPADE
IMPADE

For the dough: 1 kg of type 0 flour, 550 g of sugar,
5 eggs, 25 dl of maize seed oil.
For the filling: 500 g of sweet almonds, 500 g of sugar,
4 eggs, grated rind of 1 lemon.

To prepare these pastries, heap the flour on the pastry board and add the eggs in the middle. Knead well, gradually adding the sugar and the oil and avoiding lumps; continue kneading energetically until the mixture becomes soft and elastic, then cover and leave to rest in a bowl. Prepare the filling in the meantime.

Chop the almonds, place them in a small bowl and add the eggs, sugar and grated lemon rind, mixing carefully to amalgamate all the ingredients.

Take the dough and knead it again for a some minutes. Form it into a roll of about 2 cm in diameter and then cut into finger–length pieces. Flatten these pieces with a rolling pin into rectangles about 5 cm wide.

Place a little of the filling in the middle of each rectangle, then join the edges of the dough and press with the fingers to seal and form a small crest. Then fold one end to the right and the other to the left:, to form the typical "s–shape".

Place the "impade" on a buttered and slightly floured baking tray so that they will not touch each other as they bake. Pre–heat the oven to about 200 °C and keep this temperature for 5 minutes, then reduce to 180 °C and leave to bake for a dozen minutes before removing and leaving to cool.

"Impade" are the superb traditional desserts of the Hebrew "Easter" still today enjoyed in the Venice Ghetto area; they are also on sale in a number of bakery shops.

PEVARINI
PEVARINI

350 g of type 0 flour, 100 g of butter,
100 g of sugar, 100 g of honey, 1 spoon of mixed powdered
spices (cinnamon, nutmeg, pepper),
1 spoon of confectionery yeast, salt.

"Pevarini" were popular traditional and ancient biscuits once made by Venetian bakeries but now somewhat forgotten – although, fortunately, some bakers have recently resumed making them. "Pevarini" were once also found in certain "bàcari": "osterie" or inns serving something to eat in far from luxurious settings. In these typical places, "pevarini" and "cichéti" (snacks) were an excuse for a glass of wine (ombra) enjoyed in happy company.

Biscuits were once baked in Venice using lard instead of butter or oil, and cane sugar or molasses (treacle) in place of refined sugar. These "sweeteners" gave "pevarini" a very particular "ancient" taste and this old recipe is still valid as an alternative.

First of all, melt the butter together with the sugar and honey, add a little salt, the powdered spices (best if fresh–ground) and mix well to amalgamate all the ingredients. Add the flour and yeast, blending everything well to form a firm dough; add a drop of water, if necessary. Leave to rest for about half an hour. Then use a rolling pin to roll out the dough to a thickness of about half a centimetre. Use the tip of a knife to cut the dough into preferred shapes. Then place the biscuits on buttered oven paper on a tray, place in the oven pre–heated to about 180 °C and bake for 15–20 minutes. "Pevarini" are best enjoyed a few days after baking, accompanied by a glass of fine red wine; they keep for quite a long time provided they are closed in a glass jar or tin box.

SUCARINI
SUCARINI

*500 g of type 0 flour, 300 g of sugar, 3 eggs,
extra virgin olive oil or corn oil, grated rind
of 1/2 lemon, 50 g of refined sugar (rough–ground).*

Heap the flour on the pastry board, create a "volcano" in the middle and add the eggs. Knead, gradually adding the sugar, 3 spoons of oil and the grated lemon rind. Knead the dough well, avoiding lumps, and continue until an elastic and uniform dough is prepared.

Then roll out rather thickly and use an upside–down glass to cut disks of about 6–7 cm in diameter. Make a hole in the middle of each disk and press one side into the rough–ground refined sugar. Place the biscuits on a buttered and floured oven tray with the sugared sides upwards with enough space for baking.

Place in the oven at 180 °C and bake for about 15 minutes.

BIGARANI
BIGARANI

*500 g of fine flour, 15 g of fresh beer yeast,
100 g of sugar, 100 g of butter, 3 eggs,
1 glass of milk, salt.*

Slowly melt the butter in bain–marie. Crumble the beer yeast into lukewarm milk and allow to dissolve completely. In the meantime, beat 2 eggs and one egg yolk with a pinch di salt. Keep the remaining egg white cool.

Heap the flour on a pastry board, prepare a "volcano" and then add the beaten eggs, sugar, milk with yeast and the melted but lukewarm butter. Knead this mixture into a soft dough, then cover with a cloth and leave to rise in a lukewarm place protected against currents of air.

After about 3 hours, knead the risen dough again into finger–thick cylinders 20 cm long. Turn one tip inwards and place them on a buttered oven tray well–separated so they can

BISCOTTI E DOLCETTI
VENEZIANI

bake. Place in the oven at 150 °C and bake for about 10 minutes; Then remove the tray from the oven, brush the biscuits with the slightly beaten egg white kept apart and leave to rest overnight. The following morning, place them again in a hot oven for 10–15 minutes to biscuit the "bigarani" slightly.
Then serve with a sparkling white wine such as Prosecco di Conegliano–Valdobbiadene "superiore di Cartizze".
"Bigarani" keep for a long time provided they are kept in a tightly sealed recipient in a dry place.

In the past, "bigarani" were offered as gifts to nursing mothers – not forgetting a fine bottle of sweet wine: it was believed they would help them quickly regain their strength.
These biscuits are rather easy to make and in some way have a rather "female" appearance.

OSSI DA MORTO
DEAD MAN'S BONES

500 g of fine flour, 15 g of fresh beer yeast,
150 g of sugar, 100 g of butter, 3 eggs,
1 glass of milk, 1 small glass of aniseed, 2 spoons
of extra virgin olive oil, salt.

"Ossi da morto" can be made using several different local recipes. They are among the most popular and traditional Veneto biscuits and common all over the region, especially in the countryside around Treviso. In the past, they were "dipped" in new wine to soften them and make them even more enjoyable.
Crumble the fresh yeast in the lukewarm milk and leave to dissolve. In the meantime, melt the butter in bain–marie; beat the eggs separately for a long time with a pinch di salt, keeping aside the white of one egg.
Heap the flour into a "volcano" on the pastry board and add the beaten eggs, oil, sugar, melted butter, aniseed and milk with yeast. Knead for some time to amalgamate the ingredients completely into an even dough without lumps, then

cover with a cloth and leave to rest for 2–3 hours in a luke-warm, safe place so that it can rise.

After this time, knead the mixture again and then divide into pieces.

Roll out the pieces of dough by hand on the floured pastry board into cylinders of about 2 cm in diameter. Then cut the rolls into small cylinders about 10 cm long and press the ends inwards so that they resembles "bones".

Pre–heat the oven to a temperature of about 150 °C, place the "bones" on a buttered tray and bake for 10–15 minutes; then remove the tray from the oven, brush the biscuits with the re-maining beaten egg white and leave to set at ambient tempe–rature.

Replace the tray with the "bones" in the oven and leave to dry at moderate heat for about 30 minutes.

Accompany with a Recioto della Valpolicella dessert wine.

FAVE DEI MORTI
BEANS OF THE DEAD

*300 g of pine nuts, 200 g of sugar, 30 g of bitter cocoa,
5 egg yolks, a little flour, 1 small glass of grappa,
vanilla powder, butter.*

"Fave dei morti" are truly delicious and irresistible.
These typically Autumn biscuits are easy to prepare and are also common in other regions with slightly different ingredi-ents and doses. They are eaten in November, in the period of celebrations for the dead.

Crush the pine nuts carefully in a mortar, then blend with the sugar; lastly, add the egg yolks, cocoa, grappa and a little vanilla powder. Blend this mixture well and then form into small balls. Flatten them slightly before placing on a buttered and floured oven tray. Place in the oven at very moderate heat and bake for 10–15 minutes. Leave them to cool before eating and accompany with Recioto della Valpolicella.

AMARETI VENESSIANI
VENETIAN MACAROONS

500 g of shelled sweet almonds, 50 g of shelled bitter almonds, 500 g of sugar, 4 egg whites,
10 g of cinnamon powder, the grated peel of 2 lemons,
butter, salt.

Mince the sweet and bitter almonds in a blender and then place them in a bowl. Add the grated lemon peel (only the yellow part), sugar, cinnamon powder and a pinch di salt. Mix very well and then add the firmly beaten egg whites.
Smear an oven tray with plenty of butter. Divide the mixture into balls the size of walnuts and place them on the tray well separated so that they do not touch while baking. Flatten slightly with the palm of the hand. Then place them in an oven at moderate heat (about 170 °C) and bake for about 20 minutes, making sure that they do not become too dark.
Once baked, remove from the oven and serve cold, accompanied by Moscato dei Colli Euganei.

AMARETI E SPUMILIE

SPUMILIE
MERINGUES

200 g of vanilla sugar, 4 egg whites, flour, butter.

> Meringues are tradition desserts in certain Italian regions and very popular in the Lagoon city. Venetian pastry bakers make meringues in all kinds of shape and size and sometimes add other ingredients, such as cocoa or a little coffee. To make good meringues, the egg whites must be beaten very firmly and great care must be taken while baking them.

Pour the egg whites into a bowl previously chilled in the refrigerator for half an hour. Then beat firmly (best with an electrical whip). Then delicately blend the sieved vanilla su–gar, mixing carefully from bottom to top to keep the egg whites firm.

Butter and flour an oven tray and, using a spoon or a wide–mouth confectionery funnel, arrange the mixture in little pieces at some distance between each other.

Pre–heat the oven to about 100 °C. Place the meringues in the oven, leaving the oven door slightly open, and bake for about half an hour, making sure that they do not become too dark.

Remove from the oven, leave to cool and only then remove the meringues from the tray and arrange on a serving dish.

Then serve with a chilled sparkling white wine such as Pros–ecco di Conegliano–Valdobbiadene "Superiore di Cartizze".

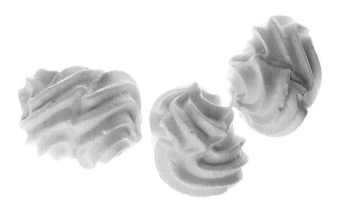

A PARE
A PARE

750 kg of type 0 flour, 600 g of sugar,
10 eggs, butter.

Separate the yolks from the egg whites and place the latter in the refrigerator in a glass bowl for at least half an hour.
Sieve the flour into another bowl and then add the sugar. Add the egg yolks and use a wooden spoon to blend the mixture very carefully. Take the bowl with the egg whites out of the refrigerator and beat very firmly. Then delicately add the bea–ten eggs whites to the previously prepared mixture. To keep the egg whites firm, blend the mixture slowly and delicately from bottom to top.
Lastly, pour spoonfuls of this mixture over a buttered and floured oven tray, making sure that the balls are well–spaced for baking. Then bake at 180 °C for about 15 minutes; remove the biscuits and leave to cool.
Serve accompanied by a good sweet wine.

"Apare" are typical and traditional Jewish Venetian biscuits prepared for the Pesach feast (Easter). These delicious biscuits are made using very few, simple ingredients used every day.

R ÉCIE DE AMAN
EARS OF AMAN

500 g of wheat flour, 50 g of sugar,
40 g of butter or margarine, 1 egg, 1 egg yolk,
1 spoon of yeast, dry white wine,
maize seed oil, icing sugar, salt.

Heap the flour on the pastry board and make a hole in the middle; add the eggs, the margarine or butter melted in a bain–marie, the sugar, a little white wine, the yeast and a pinch of salt.
Carefully knead all the ingredients, beginning with the flour on the edges of the heap to amalgamate them, then work

more firmly to achieve a soft and elastic dough. Use a rolling pin to work the dough into a very thin sheet.

Then cut out elongated ovals resembling donkey ears and fry them in plenty of boiling oil, adding them a few at time to prevent them sticking together.

Remove them from the oil using a sieved ladle and place on absorbent kitchen paper to eliminate excess oil. Lastly, sprinkle them with the icing sugar and serve.

These doughnuts – known as the "ears of Aman" – are a typical, traditional Jewish Venetian dessert prepared for the Purim feast that is also called "the feast of destiny". The event celebrates an episode narrated in the Book of Ester. During this feast, which is a rather playful occasion, it is customary to wear masks and the "récie de Aman" prepared for the celebrations are very similar to Carnival "ga'lani".

C R E M A   F R I T A
F R I E D   C R E A M

*120 g of fine flour, 120 g of sugar,
1/2 l of milk, 6 egg yolks, 1 lemon, breadcrumbs,
butter, extra virgin olive oil, fine sugar
or icing sugar for decoration, cinnamon powder
(optional), salt.*

This traditional Venetian sweet is very easy to prepare. There are several variants but here we present a simple and ancient recipe.

Beat five egg yolks in a bowl. Add and blend 80 g of sugar, then beat for some time until the mixture is foamy and clear. Add the sieved flour, grated lemon rind and a pinch of salt. Amalgamate all these ingredients very well and then add the cold milk a little at a time, blending well to avoid the formation of lumps. Place this mixture in a casserole and heat over a moderate flame while continually stirring with a wooden spoon. When the mixture comes to the boil, remove and pour into a wide tray with low edges doused with cold water. Immediately smooth off this cream using a spatula to a thickness of about 3 cm, leave to cool completely and then cut into lozenge–shaped pieces.

Beat the remaining egg yolk with a fork in a flat dish. Then dip the creamed lozenges first the beaten egg and then in the breadcrumbs, making sure they are fully coated. Prepare a pan with plenty of butter and oil and then fry the cream on all sides.

Remove the lozenges from the oil using a sieved ladle, place them on absorbent kitchen paper to dry and serve with fine sugar or icing sugar.

If preferred, you can also sprinkle with cinnamon. Serve with Moscato dei Colli Euganei or a dessert wine.

GA'LANI
GALANI

*300 g of fine flour, 120 g of sugar, 50 g of butter,
2 eggs, milk, 1 spoon of grappa, maize seed oil
or lard, 50 g of icing sugar, salt.*

Heap the flour on a pastry board and break the eggs on top. Knead with a little milk, butter softened at ambient tempera-ture, sugar, grappa and a pinch of salt. Knead all the ingre-dients into a firm yet elastic dough.

Form the dough into a ball, place it in a bowl and leave to rise covered by a slightly moistened cloth for 15 minutes in a cool place where there are no air currents.

Then use a rolling pin to prepare a very thin pastry. Then use a knife or a pastry cutter to prepare diamond–shaped pieces about two fingers thick.

Preferably using an iron pan, heat plenty of oil or, in the Venetian tradition, lard and quickly fry the "ga'lani". Remove them with a sieved ladle and sprinkle while still hot with icing sugar. Arrange in layers on a tray. The first layer in one direction, the second in the opposite direction and so forth until all the "ga'lani" are served. Be very careful since they are very fragile and may break.

Serve with a sparkling Recioto della Valpolicella.

"Ga'lani" are the traditional, delicate "fritters" of the Carnival period. Similar confectionery is found in other Italian regions: "crosto'li" in Trentino, "chiacchiere" in Lombardy, "cenci" in Tuscany, "bugie" in Piedmont, "frappe" in Umbria and so forth. Delicate, flimsy and easy to make, they are considered everywhere as the true symbol of Carnival traditions.

FRITO'LE
A'LA VENESSIANA
VENETIAN FRITTERS

400 g of type 0 wheat flour,
25 g of fresh beer yeast, 50 g of sugar, 2 eggs,
100 g of raisins/sultanas, milk, grappa, maize seed oil,
50 g of vanilla sugar, salt.

These are the popular and typical fritters of the Venetian carnival and there are many variants. This guide proposes a recipe using seed oil instead of traditional lard.

Rinse the raisins and leave them to soak in a cup with the grappa for about half an hour. Pour the flour into a bowl and blend a little milk, sugar and eggs to make a rather soft dough.

Add a little salt, the yeast dissolved in a little lukewarm water and the raisins drained and squeezed from the grappa; blend all these ingredients very carefully. Then leave the mixture in a cool, safe place to rise for about 2 hours.

When ready, heat the oil in a pan and once it begins to smoke add spoonfuls of the mixture: when the fritters become firm, turn them with a sieved ladle and leave in the pan until they become golden. Lastly, drain and leave to dry on absorbent kitchen paper.

Place the "frito'le" one by one on a serving dish and then sprinkle with vanilla sugar.

TORTA NICO'LOTA
"NICO'LOTA" CAKE

100 g of fine flour, 200 g of soft bread,
100 g of raisins/sultanas, 1 spoon of dill seeds,
1/2 l of milk, 4 spoons of extra virgin olive oil,
butter, salt.

"Nico'lota" cake takes its name from the ancient communities living on the "island" of San Nicolò dei Mendicoli, who were nicknamed "nicolotti". The inhabitants of this part of the city, until the fall of the Venetian Republic, were mostly fishermen and had very particular customs and traditions. They baked this very popular sweet that today is somewhat forgotten.

"Nico'lota" cake is made using simple ingredients going back to times when dry fruit was used in place of sugar. The only "sweeteners" in this recipe, in fact, are raisins and sultanas. Soft, fresh bread, on the other hand, was replaced by stale bread which, after being soaked in milk, ensured that left–over bread was always used up.

Break the soft bread into pieces and moisten it in lukewarm milk in a bowl. Leave the bread to soak and then squeeze slightly. Blend with the flour and washed raisins into a fairly consistent dough. Butter a tray and roll out the mixture, sprinkling the top with dill seeds. Pre–heat an oven to 170 °C and leave to bake until the cake is firm and golden.

Place on a serving dish and accompany the "nico'lota" with a good sweet wine. In the past, it was traditional to grate left–over "polenta" into the soft bread; it was also customary to use lard instead of oil and butter.

You may even add pine nuts to the dough, as well as candied citron or orange cut into small cubes.

TORTA AI PINO'LI
PINE NUT CAKE

*300 g of fine flour, 200 g of butter, 150 g of pine nuts,
50 g of walnuts, 100 g of honey, 100 g of sugar,
2 egg yolks, 2 spoons of rum.*

Remove the butter from the refrigerator and leave it to soften at ambient temperature.

Then place it in a bowl and blend with the sugar to prepare a foamy cream.

Add the egg yolks, the honey and the rum, blending all these ingredients carefully.

When well mixed, add the sieved flour a little at a time, stirring continuously with a wooden spoon. The add the walnuts, making sure they are well distributed throughout the dough. Butter a round cake dish, place half the pine nuts on the base, pour in the mixture and then sprinkle the remaining pine nuts on top. Pre–heat the oven to 180 °C and bake for 30–40 minutes. Remove from the oven and leave the cake to cool before serving.

FUGASSA DE PASQUA
EASTER CAKE

500 g of fine flour, 15 g of fresh beer yeast,
6 egg yolks, 200 g of sugar, 150 g of butter,
40 g of sweet almonds, 1/2 glass of milk, salt.

Mix one–third of the flour with the yeast dissolved in lukewarm milk in a bowl. Knead this dough into a compact form and leave to rise in a cool, safe place until it doubles in vo–lume (this will take about 2 hours).

Once this dough has risen, use a pastry board to mix the remaining flour with half the sugar and half the butter left to soften at ambient temperature. Then add the 3 egg yolks, the risen dough and a pinch of salt. Knead the dough for some time into a ball, cover with a cloth and leave to rise again for a further 2 hours. Then knead the dough again on the pastry board, gradually adding the remaining ingredients. Then co–ver again with a cloth and leave to rise for at least 3 hours. Butter a round baking tray very well, arrange the dough on it and sprinkle the top with the flaked almonds; bake at 170 °C for about one hour.

Then remove from the oven and leave to cool. Serve the "fugassa" cake with a sweet wine such as Moscato dei Colli Euganei.

FUGASSA DE PASQUA

PINSA VENESSIANA
VENETIAN "PINSA"

*300 g of yellow maize flour, 200 g of white wheat flour,
200 g of fine sugar, 200 g of butter (or lard), 100 g of
raisins/sultanas, 50 g of citron (pieces of candied citron)
and candied pumpkin,20 g of pine nuts, 5 dry figs,1 apple,
a pinch of aniseed,1/2 l of milk, 1 small glass of grappa,
1/2 a sachet of yeast powder, breadcrumbs, salt.*

Soften the raisins in lukewarm water. Dice the dried figs. Peel
the apple and cut into slices. Sieve the white flour into a
bowl, add the yeast and sugar and mix well. Pour the milk,
butter, a glass of water and a pinch of salt into a casserole;
bring to the boil and add the maize flour. Cook for 10 minutes
stirring continuously. Then blend the white flour (with yeast
and sugar) and all the other ingredients; amalgamate well and
cook for another 20 minutes, stirring continuously. Butter a
cake dish, sprinkle with breadcrumbs and then add the mixture (about two fingers deep). Bake at moderate heat (180
°C) for one hour. The "pinsa" cake is properly baked when a
brownish crust is formed. Serve still warm or cold with Recioto di Soave (white) or Recioto della Valpolicella (red).

*"Pinsa" is a dessert people begin baking when the first cold weather
arrives and is a traditional part of Christmas festivities.*
*"Pinsa" is similar to "pizza" – a substantial and satisfying dish made
using different ingredients depending on regions and personal creativity.*
*The basic ingredient is maize flour with plenty of tasty ingredients and
condiments: it was once flavoured with pork stock and sweetened
with honey or molasses because sugar was too expensive. A large por-
tion of "polenta" was prepared and wrapped in many layers of cab-
bage leaves before being cooked underneath hot charcoal. Among
country-folk, it was the "marantega" or Epiphany cake: it was baked
underneath the fires set alight on the night between 5 and 6 January,
when effigies of the old year were burnt to celebrate the end of Win-
ter and the coming arrival of Spring.*
This cake is popular in Venice and its hinterland countryside.

BUSSOLÀ
BUSSOLÀ

500 g of fine flour, 15 g of fresh beer yeast,
40 g of raisins/sultanas, 3 eggs, 1 egg yolk, 5 spoons
of sugar, 5 spoons of extra virgin olive oil,
1 spoon of grated lemon rind,
1 spoon of aniseed essence.

Although the name might be misleading, this sweet is not related to "buso'lai". It probably owes its name to its typical doughnut shape. A similar cake is also found in different Italian regions and even in other parts of Europe. It is quite easy to prepare but patience is needed since rather long rising times are involved.

First of all, dissolve the yeast in a bowl with a little lukewarm water. Add a spoonful of sugar and a little flour; then cover with a cloth and leave to rise in a cool place where there are no air currents.

Once well risen, prepare a larger bowl than before, rinse it with boiling water, dry it and, while it is still lukewarm, add the risen mixture. Add the eggs, the grated lemon rind, the re-maining sugar, oil, washed and dried raisins, half the rema-ining flour and the aniseed essence. Then mix all the ingre-dients well a wooden spoon to prepare a rather soft dough. Cover the bowl with a cloth and leave to rise in a cool place where there are no air currents, until the dough doubles in volume (this will take about 1 hour).

When the mixture has risen fully, transfer it to a floured work top or pastry board, add the remaining flour and knead for some time until a soft but consistent dough is obtained.

Form a doughnut with the classic hole in the middle and place it on a buttered and floured tray. Cover with a cloth (best if woollen), place the tray in a cool place and leave to rise again until it doubles in volume.

Lastly, smear the doughnut with the slightly beaten egg yolk and bake at about 220 °C for 5 minutes, then lower the tem-perature to 180 °C for about 40 minutes.

Traditionally, "bussolà" is enjoyed by dipping it into "zabaione" or sweet wine.

MANDO'LATO VENETO
VENETIAN ALMOND CAKE

2 kg of peeled and toasted sweet almonds, 1 kg of honey,
4 egg whites, 1 spoon of cinnamon powder, white wafers.

Heat the honey for 30 minutes over a very low heat, stirring continuously with a wooden spoon. Then leave to rest and cool for half an hour. Beat the 2 egg whites into a firm mixture. Replace the honey over a very low heat for a further 30 mi–nutes, stirring continuously, and then blend in the whipped egg whites. Take off the heat and leave to rest for another half an hour. In the meantime, firmly whip the other egg whites and prepare a broad, low recipient lined with wafers.
Replace the honey on a very low heat again, stirring continuously, and then add the other whipped egg whites. Then add the almonds and cinnamon, stirring delicately, and pour into the recipient with the wafers.
Leave to cool completely and serve "mando'lato" broken into small pieces.
Serve with a Gambellara Vin Santo (dessert wine).

MARZAPANE
MARZIPAN

1 kg of sweet almonds, 1.2 kg of sugar,
maize oil for the work top.

First of all, carefully peel the almonds. Dip them for a few seconds in boiling water and then leave them for a while in a warm oven. This will make peeling easier. On the other hand, already peeled almonds can be also used so that preparing this marzipan is quicker and easier.
Chop the almonds very finely or, better still, work them carefully with a pestle and mortar. Dissolve the sugar in a casserole

with a glass of water and then add the chopped almonds, stirring continuously with a wooden spoon.

Leave on the heat until a good consistency is obtained and then pour the mixture on to the work top (best if well–oiled marble). Use a knife to lift the edges all around, folding them inwards and repeating this operation several times until the mixture is white and sticky.

Lastly, work the marzipan with wet hands into the shapes required.

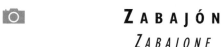

ZABAJÓN
ZABAIONE

8 egg yolks, 12 spoons of sugar, 3 dl of Marsala
or another sweet wine, cinnamon powder.

It is very easy to prepare "zabaione" but care is needed when cooking.

Pour the egg yolks and the sugar into a casserole and blend thoroughly with a wooden spoon or a whip to obtain a soft, light and foamy mixture. Add the Marsala and a little cinnamon powder, mix the ingredients and place on a very mode–rate heat, stirring continuously and always in the same dire–ction. After a while, the mixture will begin to swell and great care is needed at this point, since the "zabaione" must not come to the boil. If it does boil, the success of the recipe is compromised.

Lastly, serve hot in china cups on glass goblets, accompanied with the "baíco'li" traditionally enjoyed with this delicious speciality. If preferred, a little whipped cream can also be added. Serve cool or cold accompanied by Gambellara Vin Santo (dessert wine).

"Zabaione" is truly a very singular name, so much so that the origin of this word is unknown even among experts.

Some experts suggest that this delicious dish became popular thanks to the Venetians or, otherwise, through their contacts along the coastline of former Yugoslavia, where a thick drink (zabaja) was popular as a restorative.

Others suggest that "zabaione" derives from the Latino word (sabaia) used to indicate a type of beer. This was certainly suggsted by a visual resemblance, since the light yellow cream has a hint of a delicate foam.

In any case, an ancient Venetian custom involved preparing a concoction with eggs, sugar, Malvasia wine and a little pure alcohol, which was given to a new husband by friends at the end the wedding lunch to encourage the success of the first night.

At times, other ingredients believed to be aphrodisiacs were added, such as cinnamon, nutmeg, etc.

Today, "zabaione" is served as a dessert, accompanied by "baíco'li", or is even used to prepare other desserts.

ANTICO ZABAJÓN
ANCIENT ZABAIONE

3 eggs, 100 g of sugar, 1/2 l of dry white wine,
juice of 1 lemon.

This ancient and simple recipe, that seems to date back to the 1700s, envisages the use of fewer eggs compared to the better–known previous recipe.

Pour the wine, eggs, sugar and lemon juice into a casserole.

ZABAJÓN

Mix carefully with a wooden spoon, then place the recipient over a high heat while stirring continuously.

Just before the mixture begins to boil, remove from the heat, pour into appropriate cups and leave to cool before serving as usual with "baíco'li".

T í R A M E   s u
T I R A M I S ù

400 g of Savoy biscuits (or about 25 pieces), 6 eggs,
500 g of very fresh mascarpone, 50 g of fresh
whipped cream, 300 g of fine sugar,
3 dl of coffee, 1 small glass of kirsch (or rum),
20 g of bitter cocoa powder.

Break the eggs, placing the yolks in one bowl and the whites in another. Then whip the egg whites firmly.

Mix the egg yolks and 100 g of sugar and whip until foamy. Then also add the mascarpone, whipped egg whites, cream and the small glass of kirsch, stirring with a wooden spoon to prepare a creamy and uniform mixture.

Dissolve the remaining sugar in the coffee, then quickly dip a few Savoy biscuits before arranging them carefully on the base of a rectangular glass dish. Arrange a layer of the previously prepared cream on top; then arrange another layer of Savoy biscuits dipped in the sugared coffee, followed by another layer of cream, and so forth; finish with a well–levelled layer of cream.

Cover the glass dish with cling film and place in the refrigerator until served.

Before serving this delicious spoon dessert, sprinkle the surface with bitter cocoa powder.

Accompany with a Recioto della Valpolicella dessert wine.

The original name of this spoon dessert derives from its very high calorie content and its so–called "pick–me–up" properties.
The secret for a delicious "Tiramisù" is to use genuine and very fresh ingredients.

ROSADA
ROSADA

*1/2 l of milk, 1 stick of vanilla, 5 egg yolks,
80 g of sugar.*

Pour the milk into a casserole, bring to the boil and then add the stick of vanilla; then leave to cool off heat and remove the vanilla once cooled.

Place the egg yolks in a bowl, add the sugar and beat for some time with a whip until a soft, foamy and rather consistent mixture is formed. Slowly add the cooled milk and mix – always in the same direction – with a wooden spoon.

Pour the cream into a casserole and heat in a bain–marie, making sure that the water never comes to the boil and always stirring in the same direction. Once the mixture has thickened, take it off the heat, leave to cool and lastly pour it – in the "Venetian style" into a mould or serving goblets.

This sophisticated spoon dessert is very easy to prepare but requires delicate execution: the slow and regular movement of the hand while mixing the cream is essential. It is a dense and velvety "cream pudding" that the Venetians serve with a spoon directly from the mould. The name "rosada" refers to Spanish colours and traditions: it was once known as "Catalan Cream".

ROSADA A'LE MANDO'LE
ROSADA WITH ALMONDS

*400 g of shelled almonds, 200 g of sugar,
8 egg yolks, 5 egg whites, 6 dl of water.*

The traditional recipe obviously did not envisage using a blender – but an exception can certainly be made for conve–nience and reduce preparation times by quickly blending the almonds with water.

Then pour the almonds blended in water into a bowl, add the well–beaten egg yolks and the firmly whipped egg whites, blending everything with delicacy. Then add the sugar and mix well and very slowly. Lastly, pour into a glass dish and cook in a bain–marie in the oven until firm.

Take out of the oven, leave to cool and then serve spoonfuls from the mould in goblets.

PE'LADÈI
PE'LADÈI

1 kg of chestnuts, 1 sprig of sage, salt.

Peel the chestnuts and place in a pot covered with cold water. Add the sage and a pinch of salt. Place on the heat and boil for 45 minutes.

Serve the "pe'ladèi" hot as a dessert or a delicious afternoon snack, accompanied by a fine Recioto di Valpolicella or Recioto di Soave.

CARAMÈI
CARAMÈI

10 large grapes, 10 prunes,
10 dates, 10 walnuts, 150 g of sugar,
1 spoon of lemon juice, almond oil
or maize seed oil.

"Caramèi" are caramelised fruit. The dish is easy and rather quick to prepare; ideal for many occasions, particularly for guests with a sweet tooth or children. This recipe indicates some kinds of fruit but other fruit can also be used as preferred – such as oranges, citrons, roast chestnuts, medlars and cherries.

First of all, it is essential to procure some wooden skewers. Arrange pieces of fruit on each skewer, alternating flavours and colours.

Dissolve the sugar in the lemon juice and a little water in a casserole. Mix well and then place the casserole over the heat in a bain–marie using an appropriate recipient.

When the sugar begins to caramelise, dip the skewers of fruit so that they are completely coated. This should be done quite quickly. The skewers should then be progressively placed on a marble work top slightly moistened with almond oil or seed oil.

Leave the "caramèi" to cool completely before detaching them from the marble serve to guests on a dish still on the wooden skewers.

PERSEGADA
PERSEGADA

Quince, lemon and fine sugar.

Wash the quince, then cook in plenty of water until they become rather soft and tender. Then remove the peel and core. Place the quince pulp in a large pot and boil for some time, stirring continuously, until the mixture becomes firm.

Strain the pulp through a fine sieve, weigh it and then add the same amount of sugar. Also add the juice of one lemon for every half kilo of pulp.

Place on a low heat again and boil for 40 minutes. Take off the heat and leave to cool.

In the meantime, prepare the moulds or a low, rectangular plate lined with greaseproof paper. Add the "persegada", leave to cool for 12 hours and then leave to dry out in the open air for a day. Then turn over so that the "jam" also dries out on the other side. Lastly, cut the "persegada" into lozenge–shaped pieces and store in dry, closed recipients – they will keep for several months after preparation. Ideal with a fortified sweet wine.

POMI COTI
COOKED APPLES

6 good apples (best if somewhat bitter), 50 g of macaroons,
50 g of raisins/sultanas, 60 g of fine sugar,
30 g of butter, 1 glass of white wine, 1/2 glass
of aromatic liqueur (such as kirsch).

Wash the apples thoroughly and then completely remove the cores using an appropriate utensil (starting from the stem).
Then mix the crumbled macaroons, raisins/sultanas and half a glass of liqueur. Insert this mixture inside the cored apples and place them on a well–buttered glass dish. Sprinkle with the wine, add a knob of butter to the top of every apple and sprinkle with plenty of sugar.
Pre–heat the oven to 200 °C and bake the apples for 20–30 minutes depending on their size. Serve the filled cooked apples hot, ideally with a sweet Malvasia wine or Recioto of Soave.

BUDÍN DE RISO
RICE PUDDING

7 dl of milk, 100 g of rice, 70 g of raisins/sultanas,
50 g of pine nuts, 50 g of sugar, 1 stick of vanilla,
1 lemon, a few orange slices, salt.

Traditions in Venice (and the Veneto in general) often see rice cooked with milk and this probably has an oriental ori-

gin; rice and milk are used to make delicious soups and delightful desserts such as these "puddings". Wash the raisins/sultanas and then soften them in a little lukewarm water. In the meantime, add the milk to a casserole, warm over a moderate heat and add half a whole stick of vanilla (crumble the other half). Just before the milk comes to the boil, add the rice and, stirring continuously with a wooden spoon, leave on the heat and cook for about 15 minutes.

After this time, add a pinch of salt and the sugar, mix well and continue cooking over a low heat for about ten minutes, stirring every now and then.

Drain the raisins/sultanas, dry them and then add to the rice; also add the pine nuts and the grated lemon rind, mixing well. Remove the stick of vanilla, take off the heat and leave to rest for 5 minutes with the lid on the pot. Pour the "pudding" into buttered moulds and finish in a hot oven for a couple of minutes.

Remove the "puddings" from the oven and place on serving dishes decorated with thin slices of orange.

BUDÍN DE CIOCO'LATA
CHOCOLATE PUDDING

1/2 l of milk, 100 g of fondant chocolate, 3 egg yolks, 2 spoons of flour, 2 spoons of sugar.

Chocolate puddings were important in traditional Venetian cuisine and even Goldoni often mentioned them in his plays.

Home–made puddings prepared with simple, genuine ingredients are easy and delicious, especially for children.

Beat the egg yolks firmly in a bowl after adding the sugar and the sieved flour. This takes a few minutes to ensure that the cream is well–blended and free of lumps.

Now add the grated chocolate and the milk. Amalgamate all the ingredients carefully, pour them into a casserole and cook over a low heat. Continue whipping the mixture as it becomes slowly denser, then pour it into a mould doused with cold water. Wait until completely cooled and then turn over on to a flat plate and serve.

Accompany with fragrant "baíco'li" and a good bottle of Recioto of Gambellara.

A useful suggestion: this chocolate pudding can also be baked to improve its taste. It must be baked in a bain–marie at a temperature of about 150 °C, placing the mould with the pudding in a metal recipient with already boiling water. The level of the water must reach two thirds of the mould. Cook for 20–25 minutes, then cover with aluminium foil and leave in the oven for about 10 minutes. Then remove from the oven, leave to cool and serve.

BUDÍN DE CIOCO'LATA A'LA VANILIA

CHOCOLATE PUDDING WITH VANILLA

3/4 of l of milk, 80 g of fondant chocolate,
70 g of butter, 70 g of sugar, 50 g of flour,
1 pod of vanilla, whipped cream.

These doses are for a bigger pudding compared to the previous recipe; preparation is equally simple and the result is equally good.

Place a casserole on the heat, add the milk and bring it to the boil stirring continuously with a wooden spoon. Then remove from the heat and add the pod of vanilla.

Melt the butter in another casserole over a low flame, add the sugar, mix carefully and add the sieved flour while always stirring. As soon as the flour is blended, remove the recipient from the heat, add the crumbled fondant chocolate and a small amount of milk, while continuing to stir. Replace on a very low heat and add the rest of the milk, pouring it a little at a time into the casserole.

Bring to the boil and continue cooking for 2–3 minutes, then remove the vanilla and place the pudding in goblets moistened with cold water or a mould; then leave to cool completely.

Serve decorated with whipped cream and accompany with fragrant "baíco'li" and a good Recioto di Gambellara dessert wine.

Traditional chocolate in Venice was prepared using pure cocoa (capoè) that was dissolved in boiling water without other ingredients. A copper chocolate–making pot was used fitted with a cover incorporating a kind of windlass so that the precious and energetic drink could be stirred.

CIOCO'LATA CALDA
HOT CHOCOLATE

1/2 of water, 200 g of fondant chocolate,
50 g of sugar, 1 level spoon of cinnamon powder,
1 level spoon of maize starch, 1/2 stick of vanilla,
whipped cream (optional), salt.

The ancient recipe was rich in spices but this more recent version only includes the bouquet of cinnamon.

Grate the fondant chocolate. Dissolve the maize starch in a little lukewarm water.

Heat the water in the casserole, add the sugar and vanilla and bring to the boil.

Add the grated chocolate and dissolve it slowly, stirring with a wooden spoon. Now add the dissolved maize starch, amalgamate carefully and leave to boil for 3–4 minutes. Then remove from the heat. Add a pinch of salt and the cinnamon powder and stir well again. Then remove the stick of vanilla and serve.

Accompany the chocolate with traditional biscuits such as "baíco'li" or whipped cream.

ROSOLIO
ROSOLIO

40 g of fresh red rose petals, 1.6 kg of sugar,
1.4 l of 90° alcohol, 1.2 l of water.

Work the rose petals carefully with a marble pestle and mortar. When the petals are pulped, add 100 gr. of sugar. Conti–nue working until a red paste is formed; then leave it to ma–cerate for 10 days in the alcohol in a glass jar. Place the water and sugar in a casserole and heat.
Slowly dissolve the sugar without bringing it to the boil and then leave to cool.
Add this syrup to the glass jar with the rose mixture, mix, seal and leave to rest for a further 10 days.
After this time, filter the mixture carefully, pour into bottles, seal and store in a cool, dark place.

In the past, "rosolio" was not only enjoyed in homes or salons but also served in Venice at the tables of the legendary Caffé Florian to its famous and variegated clientele. This famous coffee house was a crossroads of news and gossip in the city and the famous Venetian playwright Goldoni, who was a regular client and shrewd observer of social customs, mentions this delicate and agreeable liqueur in his works. Florian was also the only such place in its times to allow women to enter, who already then enjoyed this sophisticated pink liqueur.

R O S O L I O   R O S S O
RED ROSOLIO

200 g of red rose petals, 800 kg of sugar,
7 dl of 90° alcohol, 6 l of water.

This is a variant of the previous recipe. In this case, a much larger quantity of rose petals is used to make a "rosolio" with a more evident aroma and more intense colour.

Work the rose petals carefully with a marble pestle and mortar. A blender can also be used. In either case, a red paste is produced which should be placed in a glass jar. Add the alcohol to the jar and leave to macerate for 10 days.

After this time, dissolve the sugar in slightly heated water to form a transparent syrup and then leave it to cool. Add the cold syrup to the maceration jar, seal and shake the recipient once a day for 40 days.

Lastly, filter the mixture – squeezing the petal paste well – then pour into bottles and keep in a cool, dark place for at least a month before tasting this aromatic "rosolio".

R O S O L I O   D I   C H I O D I
D I   G A R O F A N O
ROSOLIO WITH CLOVES

50 g of cloves, 10 g of cinnamon,
5 g of coriander seeds, 1.7 kg of sugar,
1 l of 85° alcohol, 1 l of water.

This "rosolio" recalls the perfumes of the Orient and has a particular, spicy taste that is very unusual and agreeable.

Work cloves, coriander and cinnamon carefully with a marble pestle and mortar. Then place the ground spices in a glass jar and the alcohol. Seal and leave to macerate for 8 days.

After this time, prepare a syrup: dissolve the sugar in slightly heated water to make a transparent liquid, then leave it to cool before adding it to the other ingredients. Then seal again and leave to rest for 2 days.

Lastly, filter carefully through a thin gauze, squeezing the poultice of spices well to extract all the liquid. Pour into bottles and leave to rest in a cool, dark place. Wait at least a month before tasting.

R ATAFIÀ DI CILIEGIE
C HERRY RATAFIÀ

*700 g of ripe cherries, 400 g of sugar,
250 g of 95° alcohol, 1 l of grappa.*

Clean and dry the cherries, remove the stems and pips but keep the latter aside.
Arrange the cherries in a glass recipient with an hermetic seal and cover with grappa. Work half the pips with a pestle and

mortar and then place them in another recipient, covering this time with the alcohol. Seal the two recipients and leave them in the Sun for 30 days, only bringing them inside overnight.

Shake the jar containing the pips once a day.

After this time, prepare the syrup with 100 g of water and the sugar, boil for a few minutes to dissolve the sugar, then leave to cool.

Filter the liquid of the two recipients into a single recipient, add the cold syrup of sugar, shake well, filter again and then pour into bottles; seal the bottles well and store in the cellar.

After a month, the cherry ratafià will be ready for tasting – it is traditionally served in precious, small arabesque glasses.

RATAFIÀ DI FRAGOLE
STRAWBERRY RATAFIÀ

1.1 kg of strawberries, 600 g of sugar,
0.75 l of 90° alcohol, 1/2 l of water.

This recipe requires very fresh, firm and ripe strawberries.

Remove the stems from the strawberries and, where possible, avoid washing them.

If they are soiled, immerse them rapidly in water, drain and leave to dry on plenty of absorbent kitchen paper, then leave them for some time in the Sun or an airy place.

Now place the clean strawberries in a large glass jar, add the alcohol and leave to macerate for 8 days.

After this time, pour off the pink liquid formed into another glass jar, then squeeze the remaining strawberries through a gauze to add their liquid to the other.

Dissolve the sugar in slightly heated water to form a transparent syrup and then leave it to cool.

Add the cold syrup to the alcoholic liquid, mix carefully and seal the jar.

Wait for a few days and then filter again into bottles, seal well and keep in a cool, dark place; wait for at least a month before tasting.

In the early 1600s, Venice was the most important port trading coffee in Europe, undoubtedly thanks to its great tradition of contacts with the Orient. This is why St. Mark's Square in 1683 saw the creation of the first Coffee House.

And "Bottega del Caffé" (The Coffee House) is also one of the most important plays by Carlo Goldoni, written in 1750.

The author's intention was not to represent a specific event but to paint a picture of Venice and the life of the people who frequented this place. The entire play is none other than a "slice of life" transposed into theatre and audiences at the time would have easily recognised themselves. The figures of interest to Goldoni were members of the middle classes and embodied the daily goings on and rituals he staged exactly as in real life. It is no coincidence that everything revolves around the Coffee House, the place frequented by customary clients, passersby, illustrious Venetians, intellectuals and – of course – incorrigible timewasters!

MAROCHÍN A'LA VENESSIANA
MOROCCAN

1 espresso coffee, sweet cocoa, foamy milk, grappa, cinnamon powder.

A delicious and energetic hot drink with a vaguely exotic taste. It is best served in a glass with a metal handle similar to those used to serve hot punch. Prepare an espresso coffee and pour it into the glass, add a spoon of grappa, sprinkle with cocoa and add the thick foam of milk. Sprinkle again with cocoa and cinnamon powder.

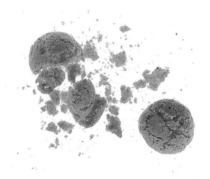

Printed in January 2009
by EBS Editoriale Bortolazzi-Stei
San Giovanni Lupatoto (Verona)
Italy